MONSTERS

GRIFFINS

BY BONNIE JUETTNER

KIDHAVEN PRESS

A part of Gale, Cengage Learning

GALE
CENGAGE Learning™

Detroit • New York • San Francisco • New Haven, Conn • Waterville, Maine • Lon

GALE
CENGAGE Learning‴

LIBRARY OF CONGRESS CATALOGING-IN-PUBLICATION DATA

Juettner, Bonnie.
  Griffins / by Bonnie Juettner.
    p. cm. — (Monsters)
  Includes bibliographical references and index.
  ISBN 978-0-7377-4043-1 (hardcover)
  1. Griffins—Juvenile literature. I. Title.
  BL325.G7J84 2008
  398'.469—dc22

2008007970

KidHaven Press
27500 Drake Rd
Farmington Hills MI 48331

ISBN-13: 978-0-7377-4043-1
ISBN-10: 0-7377-4043-4

in the United States of America
6 7 12 11 10 09 08

CONTENTS

CHAPTER 1

KING OF BEASTS AND SKY

The lion is often called the "king of the beasts." The eagle is called the "king of the air." What creature could rule both beasts and air? The ancient Greeks and Romans believed such an animal could be found deep in the deserts of central Asia. This animal was a cross between a lion and an eagle. It had four legs, like a lion, but was covered in feathers, like a bird. It was said to have eyes like fire, razor-sharp claws, and the beak and wings of an eagle. It may have also had a frill around its neck. Some writers thought it was covered in feathers. They said that its feathers were mostly black. It also had red feathers on its breast and blue feathers in patterns around its neck. Others thought

As a cross between a lion and an eagle, the griffin is considered to be one of the most majestic animals in mythology.

it was covered with spotted fur, like a leopard. Either way, it was the most majestic of all the mythological animals: the griffin.

TREASURE HOARDS

Ancient peoples believed that griffins lived in **Scythia**, a part of the world we now know as central Asia. Scythia included the present-day countries of Kazakhstan, Ukraine, Azerbaijan, Georgia, Belarus, Bulgaria, and parts of Russia and Poland. This part of the world was known for its mineral riches, especially gold and precious gems. Griffins were thought to mine for gold using their strong beaks, and they had a reputation as fierce guardians of gold mines.

Griffins, as animals, would not have had any use for gold. Ancient scholars wondered why they would bother to guard it. Some thought that griffins made their nests high in the mountains and then lined their nests with gold. They would then guard their nests, because the nests contained eggs and, eventually, baby griffins. Pliny the Elder, a Roman writing in A.D. 77, did not think that griffins put gold in their nests on purpose. Instead, he wrote, they accidentally tossed up gold when they dug holes to make burrows.

Some ancient scholars thought that griffins did not lay eggs, like other birds—instead they laid precious gems. Some said they laid agates, an especially beautiful type of quartz. Others claimed that griffins laid sapphires.

One-Eyed Giants

According to the stories, griffins were not the only monster to live in Scythia. Scythia was also the home of the **cyclops,** a one-eyed giant. Greek and Roman myths tell how griffins constantly fought with the one-eyed people of Scythia (called the

Legend says that like the griffin, the cyclops, or one-eyed giant, also lived in Scythia and that the griffins and cyclops people would often fight over gold.

"one-eyed Arimaspians") over gold. Cyclops miners would set out at night, partly because they hoped the griffins would not see them, but also to avoid hot temperatures during the day. The one-eyed Arimaspians always rode horses, and griffins became notorious for their hatred of horses. Of course, like the griffins, the cyclops people were not real. But the real people of central Asia also rode horses.

If a griffin fought with a cyclops, who would win? Ancient myths tell us that the griffin was fierce enough to best almost any other animal, even a dragon. But they refused to fight with lions or elephants. A Roman author, Philostratos, wrote that griffins could not fly very far at a time, but that they could fight from the air. He said they could revolve their feet in order to use their sharp claws. However, Philostratos said, a griffin could not possibly win a fight with a tiger, because tigers are as fast as the wind. Ordinary humans had no hope of killing or capturing a fully grown griffin. They could, however, capture a young griffin—but only if they were able somehow to get past its extremely protective parents.

Mistaken Historians

Today we think of these stories as myths. But the ancient Greeks and Romans thought of them as history or science. Herodotus, an ancient Greek historian who today is often called the "father of history," wrote about griffins in the fifth century B.C. He said that griffins hoard their gold from one-eyed men who try to steal it. Pliny the Elder, an ancient Roman historian, wrote about them too, hundreds of years later. Modern historians and scientists have checked many of the facts in the works of both Herodotus and Pliny. These ancient scholars were right about a lot of things, but not about griffins.

GRIFFIN SKELETONS

Why were ancient scholars so sure that griffins were real? They may have seen skeletons or talked to people who had seen skeletons. Ancient peoples often found dinosaur bones. When they found full skeletons, they did the same thing that scientists do with skeletons today—they tried to put them together.

One kind of dinosaur, a **protoceratops**, was common in central Asia. The skull of a protoceratops has a beak like a bird. But protoceratops also has four legs and a tail—like a lion. A protoceratops skeleton looks like a cross between a bird and a large cat. It also has a frill around its neck. Today some scientists believe that ancient peoples may have thought protoceratops was a griffin. They were partly right. Scientists now believe that dinosaurs were related to birds. It would not be wrong to describe a dinosaur as a bird with four legs—which is exactly what ancient peoples thought griffins were.

In the same area where people found the protoceratops skeletons, they probably also fou

Protoceratops skeletons and skulls, like the one pictured here, may have been mistaken by ancient peoples to be those of griffins.

mammoth skeletons. A mammoth was a prehistoric elephant with long hair and long tusks. But mammoths had been extinct for at least 2,000 years the time that ancient Ukrainians and Kazakhs began finding their bones. Today scientists think that people who did not know about mammoths could have thought that the bones they found actually came from human giants.

How is it possible to mistake a mammoth for a giant? It is possible to lay out a mammoth skeleton so that it looks like a giant human. To people who did not know they were looking at the skeleton of a four-legged animal, the mammoth's leg bones may have appeared to be arm and leg bones. A mammoth skull looks surprisingly human. One big difference between human and mammoth skulls, though, is that a mammoth skull has a large hole where its trunk was attached to its head. To people who did not know they were looking at a mammoth skull, this hole may have looked exactly like the one eye of a cyclops.

Fear of Skeletons

Dinosaurs became extinct millions of years before any humans lived on Earth. Mammoths lived millions of years after the dinosaurs, but were extinct more than 2,000 years before people began to write about the griffin and the cyclops. But ancient people did not have any way to figure out how old a skeleton was. They probably thought that the skeletons they found came from two species that still existed. They may have watched closely for griffins and for one-eyed giants—and journeyed by night to avoid attacks—whenever they traveled through the area.

Although ancient peoples feared griffins, they also admired them. Griffins were thought to be fierce guardians. Instead of trying to think of ways to kill griffins, people began to imagine what powerful friends the griffins might be. Griffins, they thought, ought to be the friends of kings, or the servants of the gods.

CHAPTER 2

FRIENDS OF KINGS AND GODS

Alexander the Great was a king who conquered all of the land between Greece and India. He lived in the fourth century B.C. After he died storytellers told many tales about him. One story was that he tried to conquer the sky as well as the land. He captured griffins and starved them for three days. Then he harnessed the griffins to his chariot with iron chains. He used long sticks to hold out meat in front of them, to tease them into flying. According to the story, they did fly, but foggy weather forced them to land again. Alexander was left stranded, a ten-day march away from his army.

In another version of this story, Alexander wanted to see God. He tried to get the griffins to fly

 Griffins

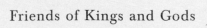

Griffins have been used in
stories as servants to gods
and kings, such as
Alexander the Great.

him up to heaven. He flew straight up for seven days. Then he met an angel who asked him why he wanted to see heaven when he did not yet understand Earth. Embarrassed, Alexander flew back down.

Alexander was a real king who was important in history. But the story of how he harnessed griffins to his chariot is a legend. In many legends griffins appear as the servants of kings or the allies of gods.

The Hounds of Zeus

Griffins appear in several Greek legends as servants to the gods. Some stories tell of how Prometheus, the god who brought fire to humans, was punished by Zeus. Prometheus was chained to a rock, and every day birds came to peck out his liver. Every night his liver grew back. In some versions of the story, the birds that peck at Prometheus are griffins. Other legends tell how griffins worked for the gods Apollo and Dionysus. Apollo was the Greek god of light. He was said to ride on a griffin, and griffins guarded his treasure for him. In Indian versions of this legend, griffins pull the sun across the sky every day. Dionysus was the god of wine. He had a bowl from which wine flowed out endlessly, and griffins guarded the bowl for him. And in some Egyptian and Persian stories, the gods appear in the forms of griffins themselves, instead of having griffin companions.

In ancient times, though, griffins appeared more in art than they did in stories. They were used as

A section of King Ahiram's sarcophagus shows a griffin providing protection to the king.

statues outside the temples of Greek gods for hundreds of years. Typically a temple sculpture would show a cauldron, with griffins attached to the rim from the bases of their long necks. Paintings from Mycenae often show religious processions in which a bull is guarded by griffins and lions.

Griffins were also used to decorate funeral urns and the walls of tombs. Here, too, they tended to appear as the protectors of kings. For example, the tomb of Lebanon's King Ahiram is from the 13th century B.C. It is decorated with a griffin attacking

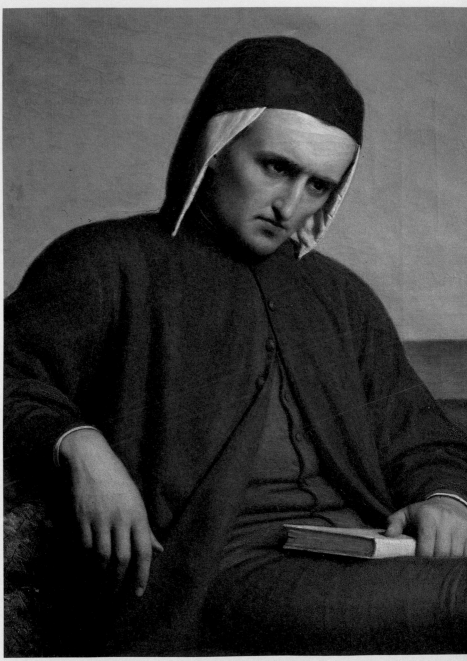

Scholars now believe that the Italian poet Dante, pictured, used a griffin to symbolize Jesus Christ in one of his works.

Griffins

a bull, and it contains a disk covered with leaping griffins. In central Asia, tombs sometimes contained horse bridles and stalls that were decorated with griffins. Archaeologists have also found griffin murals in throne rooms from Crete to Russia. Griffins are often shown sitting next to the king.

Griffins also appear on the sides of chariots and on shields. Usually the griffin is on the side of the king, protecting him. But one Russian painting shows a huntsman on an elephant fighting with two griffins. The huntsman is thought to be the god Indra, while the griffins are thought to represent evil forces that Indra struggles to defeat.

COATS OF ARMS

During the Middle Ages, knights in armor also carried shields that had griffins painted on them. Griffins on shields were very fierce looking. They were shown rearing up. Usually they faced left. They stood on one hind leg, while lifting the other three legs in the air. Griffins were said to have the ability to fight with three legs at once. Some scholars today think that knights used griffins on their shields in order to frighten their opponents' horses. Griffins and horses were believed to be mortal enemies. But others think that a knight bearing a griffin on his shield was claiming to be as strong and brave as a griffin. Knights may have also thought carrying the griffin would show that a knight had the strength of a lion and the swiftness of an eagle.

Either way, griffins in the Middle Ages were generally used to stand for the side of good. They were used to decorate Christian churches and cathedrals. Sometimes griffins were used to stand for Jesus or for the Church. In the 13th century, Dante wrote a long poem telling the story of what it would be like to descend into hell and then climb out again. As he climbs out of hell, he is met by a procession. At the head of the procession is a griffin pulling a chariot. Dante, like other poets, tended to use animals and other images as **symbols** for ideas that are hard to understand. Scholars today think that Dante's griffin is a symbol for Jesus, while his chariot is a symbol for the Church.

DRINKING FROM A CLAW

People in the Middle Ages thought that griffins were, if not holy, at least good and noble animals. Some thought that a griffin's claw could be used to heal people. They also thought that a griffin's feather could restore the sight of a blind person. People drank out of cups made from what they thought were griffin claws (they were probably actually antelope horns). They hoped the griffin claw cups would purify the liquid within. Some thought that poison, if it were served in a griffin claw, would change color.

Some people in the Middle Ages thought that it was possible to trick griffins into helping people. At some time between 1159 and 1173, Benjamin of Tudela traveled from Europe to China. When he returned he told the story of how Chinese sailors tried to trick the griffins that live around the Sea of Nikpa. He said that when their ships wrecked on islands in that sea, the sailors would cover themselves with animal skins. Griffins were thought to be meat eaters. When griffins who were out hunting for food saw the sailors from the sky, they would mistake the sailors for animals. They would swoop down, pick the sailors up, and carry them to nests on the mainland. Then the sailors could try to escape from the griffin nests and make their way home.

People in the Middle Ages also collected griffin eggs, which were probably really ostrich eggs. It would have been easy to mistake an ostrich egg for a griffin egg, because people thought that griffin eggs would be about the same size as ostrich eggs. They also believed that a person might find a griffin's nest by looking for certain things. A female griffin who was about to lay eggs would look for a cave with a narrow entrance but plenty of room inside. She would lay three eggs at a time. It would take a brave person to go out hunting for griffin eggs, because mother griffins defended their nests to the death. People admired the mother griffin's protectiveness toward her eggs. They also admired griffins' loyalty to their mates. They believed that griffins mated for life. If a griffin's mate died, it would never mate again. Instead it would live alone for the rest of its life.

People in the Middle Ages may have mistakenly collected ostrich eggs, like the ones pictured here, instead of griffin eggs, which really did not exist.

Griffins

Ancient and medieval authors used stories about griffins to try to make a point. They wanted to inspire people to be like griffins—strong, noble, brave, loyal, and good. Later, authors lost interest in using griffins as symbols for good. Instead they decided to write about griffins that were like people. In these stories every griffin is unique.

Chapter 3

Protector of Wizards

In 2001 author Tamora Pierce brought griffins to life for young adults in *Squire*, the second book of her Protector of the Small series. Kel, a squire in training to become a knight, rescues an animal from bandits. She is alarmed to discover that the animal she rescued is a baby griffin. In Pierce's books griffin parents can detect the smell of their child on anyone who has handled it, even years later, and will tear that person to shreds. Kel fears for her life, but she takes care of the baby griffin.

Even caring for a baby griffin is a dangerous job. As Kel hand-feeds the baby, it accidentally bites her and claws her fingers. She tries feeding it with a gloved hand, but it refuses to eat. Eventually she has scars on every finger. She cannot keep the griffin in a cage, because griffins have the ability to rust metal quickly so that it falls apart. Luckily Kel eventually is able to return the griffin to its parents with the help of a magician who can talk to griffins.

BRINGING GRIFFINS TO LIFE

Today scientists and historians no longer believe that griffins are real animals. Griffins are imaginary, like unicorns and fairies. However, this does not mean that authors cannot continue to write about them. Instead it means that authors can use their imaginations to come up with more details about what griffins might be like. They can write about talking griffins, griffins with magical abilities, or griffins that help adventurers accomplish their quests.

When Tamora Pierce wrote about Kel's experiences with the baby griffin, she imagined what it would be like to take care of such a fierce animal. She described how Kel had to protect herself by wearing leather clothing and learning to trim griffin claws. She also gave griffins magical abilities, such as the ability to rust metal and the ability to live forever. Books that contain magical, imaginary creatures are part of a genre called **fantasy**.

Tamora Pierce is not the only fantasy author to bring griffins to life. In *Dark Lord of Derkholm* and *Year of the Griffin*, Diana Wynne Jones imagined a magician who likes to invent new animals. The

Authors and artists use vivid details to bring griffins to life. This is clearly shown in this tapestry of the mythical creature fighting a panther.

magician uses cells from his own body and his wife's body when he invents griffins, so that his griffin creations will also be his children. As a result several of the griffins inherit his ability to do magic and become wizards. Wynne Jones's griffins are much like human teenagers. But they still keep the mythological griffin's ability to scare people with their sharp beaks and claws. In Debi Gliori's books *Pure Dead Magic, Pure Dead Wicked,* and their sequels, a griffin character is one of the family pets. It lives in the cellar and has the ability to turn itself into stone, like a gargoyle, and then turn itself back again.

TALKING GRIFFINS

Another fantasy author, Gillian Bradshaw, has brought both griffins and their enemy, the one-eyed Arimaspians, back to life. In her book *Beyond the North Wind,* she writes about a real Greek author, Aristeas. Aristeas was a poet. He visited Scythia in real life and wrote about what he had learned about griffins and the one-eyed Arimaspians.

Aristeas's poem has been lost. We only know about it because Herodotus mentions it in his *Histories.* But Bradshaw imagined what Aristeas's visit to Scythia might have been like. Herodotus said that Aristeas was a magician. And Bradshaw thought of a way for Aristeas to do his magic, by using music and playing a **lyre**. She made him a dedicated servant of the god Apollo and gave him the ability to do magic that would heal people, not hurt them. Bradshaw gives Aristeas the ability to talk to griffins using telepathic communication, passing thoughts and images from mind to mind without using words.

Unlike Bradshaw, most authors who give griffins the ability to speak let them use their beaks to speak aloud, instead of having them speak mind to mind. One of the first writers to imagine a talking griffin was Lewis Carroll, who wrote *Alice in Wonderland* and *Through the Looking Glass*. Carroll's griffin is spelled **gryphon**. (*Griffin* can be spelled in several ways, including *griffin, gryphon, griffon,* etc.) Carroll's gryphon has a sharp beak and claws, but it does not appear to be fierce. It takes Alice to meet the Mock Turtle and has a long conversation with her. Instead of attacking Alice physically, with its claws, Carroll's gryphon attacks with words. It calls Alice a simpleton and tells her she ought to be ashamed of herself for asking simple questions.

HIPPOGRIFFS

One fantasy author, J.K. Rowling, has taken griffin mythology one step further. In *Harry Potter and the Prisoner of Azkaban* she introduces a related species, the **hippogriff**. According to Greek and Roman mythology, hippogriffs are very rare. They are the children that are born when a griffin mates with its archenemy, the horse. According to Rowling, though, hippogriffs are from Europe and can be found worldwide.

Harry Potter author J.K. Rowling introduced the hippogriff, a species related to the griffin, in her book Harry Potter and the Prisoner of Azkaban.

Although they are descended from griffins, hippogriffs do not have any lionlike body parts. Instead, a hippogriff has the head, wings, and front legs of an eagle and the body, hind legs, and tail of a horse. Like griffins, though, they are extremely dangerous.

Unlike the griffins in other fantasy novels, hippogriffs in the world of Harry Potter do not talk. But they have their own way of communicating. In *The Prisoner of Azkaban*, Harry learns that hippogriffs are easily offended. To approach one, a wizard must walk toward it and bow. The wizard must also maintain eye contact without blinking. Hippogriffs do not trust people who blink too much. If the hippogriff bows in return, the wizard may touch it. If the hippogriff does not bow, the wizard should back off. If insulted, a hippogriff may attack, so wizards must be careful what they say. Though they do not talk, hippogriffs in Rowlings's books seem to understand what is said to them.

Although Harry Potter does not get to meet a griffin, Rowling says they exist in her book *Fantastic Beasts & Where to Find Them.* There, she says that some wizards have become friends with griffins. Sometimes griffins work for wizards, guarding their treasure.

Griffins in books almost always live in a world of fantasy and magic. But in the real world, griffins have another reputation. Sometimes they do appear in a fantastic world, such as the world of video games and role-playing. But now they also stand for the unique, cutting edge parts of science and technology.

CHAPTER 4

GRIFFINS RISE AGAIN

A plane glides by, 2.5 miles (4km) above the surface of the Earth. A door on the side of the plane opens, and out jumps something with long black wings. It does not plummet to Earth. Instead it flies, silently, swiftly, at speeds of 124 miles per hour (200kph). It is a modern gryphon.

GRYPHON SKYDIVERS

These new gryphons were designed by Germany's armed forces. These gryphons are actually human paratroopers—soldiers who jump out of planes and land using parachutes. They have 6-foot-long wings (1.8m) made out of carbon fibers. Normally when a paratrooper jumps out of a plane, he or she must go into **free fall**, dropping like a stone. But the gryphon soldiers do not go into free fall. Instead they fly, like a plane. They can fly 120 miles (193km) in nearly total silence, carrying up to 44 pounds (20kg) of gear. Radar could detect them, but most radar does not. Most radar systems are programmed to ignore smaller flying objects. So the gryphon paratroopers can glide into an area unnoticed.

When the gryphons land, they still must use parachutes. Before deploying the parachutes, they dis-connect the long carbon wings. The wings stay con-nected to the paratrooper with a tether, but they stay a short distance away. At the same time, a parachute deploys, slowing the paratrooper's progress toward Earth. That way, he or she can land safely.

The gryphon paratroopers are typical of the griffin's new image. Today griffins are a symbol. They stand for superior technology, and sometimes for awesome speed. They also stand for unique-ness. When people use the griffin symbol, they are trying to say that something is creative and unique. It is like nothing else that has existed before.

GRIFFON ROBOTS

The designers of the German gryphon admired the mythical griffin's ability to fly and to fight. Some re-searchers in the United States feel the same way about griffins. They have designed a robot **Griffon** (this is another common spelling for *griffin*). The

 Griffins

An unmanned aerial vehicle (UAV) is shown flying in formation beneath an F-18 aircraft. U.S. researchers have developed a Griffon UAV similar to the one pictured here.

Griffon can take off, fly at speeds of about 20 miles per hour (32kph), and land. It can be operated by remote control and could fly over land that would be hard for people to cross. For example, it could fly over lakes and mountains.

Researchers hope it could be used by the U.S. military as an unmanned aerial vehicle (UAV). It could carry cameras to be used to survey an area. It could carry weapons, such as bombs. Or it could be used in a search-and-rescue operation to carry supplies to people who are stranded.

Fear the Griffon

In 2007 engineers finished building a griffin roller coaster that can zoom at speeds of 71 miles per hour (114kph). It dives straight down from a height of 205 feet (62.5m). This griffin is located at Busch Gardens Europe, an amusement park near Williamsburg, Virginia. It is designed to scare and thrill its riders. At first designers named it Iron Eagle. Then they changed the name to Volture. Finally they settled on Griffon.

Like other products named after griffins, the Griffon is unique. It is a dive-machine coaster. This means that some sections of the roller coaster's track go straight down at a 90 degree angle. Some people call this kind of coaster a vertical-drop coaster. There are other vertical-drop coasters in the United States, but the Griffon is said to be the fastest. It also features the world's longest drop.

Courage Needed

Just to make the Griffon more frightening, its designers made it floorless. Riders travel on a series of seats that are connected together. But there is no scaffolding around the riders—no floor, no ceiling, and no walls. Riders in a roller coaster are subject to the forces of acceleration. These forces are called **g-forces**. One g-force equals the amount of acceleration you would feel from Earth's gravity if you fell. The Griffon subjects its riders to four g-forces. It also inverts them, or turns them upside down, twice.

Fighting Aircraft

Sometimes a griffin symbol refers to more than just a product's uniqueness. Sometimes it is meant to show that a product combines the qualities of two different things in one, just as the griffin combines the qualities of the lion and the eagle in one animal. Saab, a Swedish manufacturer, uses the griffin as its symbol. Saab makes both aircraft and cars. Its cars are designed to give the driver the feeling of being a pilot.

However, Saab has also developed an aircraft named after the griffin. It is called the *Gripen*, which means "griffin" in Swedish. The Gripen is a fighting aircraft. It can engage in air battles with other aircraft. It can attack soldiers on the ground. Or it can do spy missions. The Gripen is more flexible

The Swedish manufacturer Saab uses a griffin as its logo. Since Saab produces both cars and aircraft, it wants a reputation as king of land and air, like the griffin.

than most aircraft because it does not need to land or take off from a runway. It can, if necessary, land or take off from a public highway. Saab has sold the Gripen to several countries for their armed forces. Czech Republic, Hungary, South Africa, Sweden, and the United Kingdom all have Gripen fighters in their national air forces.

Other Griffins in Modern Life

Griffins are not always used to show military might and daring. Sometimes they are used to stand for superiority and nobility. Several colleges use the griffin as their symbol or school mascot. For example, Reed College, Purdue, Missouri Western State University, Sarah Lawrence, Marymount Manhattan, and the Cambridge School of Weston all have griffins as their symbol. To students at these schools, the griffin stands for a superior education. It may also stand for the wisdom students gain from their education.

One award, the Gryphon Award for Children's Literature, uses the griffin to stand for creativity and originality. It awards $1,000 to writers who write books for children who are learning to read. Like the griffin, these children can be said to have two natures. They still enjoy having adults read to them. But they are also learning to be independent readers.

Of course, modern griffins are no more real than the mythological griffins were. A roller coaster, however terrifying, is not a winged beast. A gryphon paratrooper, however awe inspiring, is really a human with a parachute. Sometimes people want to see real griffins. When they do, they may choose to use their imaginations and read novels. Or they may go to museums and galleries that include griffin paintings and sculptures. Another option

The Sandman series by graphic novelist Neil Gaiman includes a griffin as one of its characters.

is to play video games and role-playing games that include griffin characters. Some people read comic books and graphic novels like Neil Gaiman's The Sandman series, which includes a griffin character. Perhaps there are real griffins somewhere, living in a remote, unexplored wilderness. But until humans discover such a beast, people who want to see griffins have only one place to turn—the world of fantasy.

GLOSSARY

cyclops: A one-eyed giant that was said to live in Scythia and fight with the griffin over gold.

fantasy: A type of book or story that contains magic, imaginary creatures, or other elements that would not normally be found in real life.

free fall: The condition of falling from an airplane before opening a parachute.

g-forces: Acceleration forces, such as the forces that riders in a roller coaster experience.

Griffon: The name used for a military robot that can fly and be operated by remote control; also the name of a roller coaster.

gryphon: The same animal as a griffin, but spelled differently.

hippogriff: The offspring of a griffin and its arch-enemy, the horse.

lyre: A small, stringed, U-shaped musical instrument used in ancient Greece.

mammoth: A prehistoric elephant with long hair and long tusks.

protoceratops: A type of dinosaur commonly found in central Asia that has a birdlike beak, a frill around its neck, and four legs and a tail.

Scythia: Central Asia, including the present-day countries of Kazakhstan, Ukraine, Azerbaijan, Georgia, Belarus, Bulgaria, and parts of Russia and Poland.

symbols: Images that are used to stand for ideas, especially ideas that are hard to understand.

FOR FURTHER EXPLORATION

BOOKS

Pierre Grimal. *The Dictionary of Classical Mythology.* Oxford, UK: Blackwell Reference, 1996. A reference book that explains mythological references. Includes entries on monsters, gods, and heroes from classical mythology.

Joe Nigg, *Wonder Beasts: Tales and Lore of the Phoenix, the Griffin, the Unicorn, and the Dragon.* Englewood, CO: Libraries Unlimited, 1995. Includes little-known stories, legends, and myths about each animal.

Philip Wilkinson, *Illustrated Dictionary of Mythology: Heroes, Heroines, Gods, and Goddesses from Around the World.* New York: DK, 2006. Includes the basic facts about and lavish illustrations of many different mythological creatures, including the griffin and the cyclops.

WEB SITES

Encyclopedia Mythica (www.pantheon.org/). An online encyclopedia of mythology, folklore, and religion. Includes the mythologies of Africa, the Americas, and Asia, as well as classical Greek and Roman mythology.

Griffins in Art and on the Web (www.isidore-of-seville.com/griffins/). A history of art through griffins, packed with images of griffins.

The Gryphon Pages (www.gryphonpages.com). A review of research and literary references to griffins. Includes pages on modern and ancient literature and pages on art and architecture.

INDEX

PICTURE CREDITS

ABOUT THE AUTHOR

Bonnie Juettner is a writer and editor of children's reference books and educational videos. She loves fantasy novels, especially when they contain griffins. Originally from McGrath, Alaska, she currently lives in Kenosha, Wisconsin. This is her thirteenth book.